Do You Believe In Angels ?

You Should…

True life experiences and guidance with
never before seen Photographs.

Written by Susan Cormack

AuthorHouse™ UK Ltd.
500 Avebury Boulevard
Central Milton Keynes, MK9 2BE
www.authorhouse.co.uk
Phone: 08001974150

First published by AuthorHouse 2/9/2009

ISBN: 978-1-4389-3335-1 (sc)

Printed in the United States of America
Bloomington, Indiana

This book is printed on acid-free paper.

authorHOUSE®

This Book is Dedicated to

My Three Wonderful Children
Matt, Samantha, Ronan, hard work
But worth every ounce.
Also my parents Helen & Tommy
Without them many struggles would
Have been much harder to deal with.

May the Angel's always keep you safe.

Love and Light

Always

Introduction to the Author

Myself I am a very ordinary woman, qualified in child care but have done a few occupations over the years.

I am a lone parent, have been divorced once and have a failed relationship, my two older children were born when I was married, my youngest son is from my relationship.

I am a full-time carer and mum to my special needs daughter as well as caring for my two sons, we live in a rented cottage in Midlothian, Scotland.

I have clairaudience, claircognizance, clairvoyance, i work with Angels and Archangels, I give guidance, healing and work with crystals and stones.

My experiences with Angels over the years have been in obundance although were not always obvious to me at the time.

But since the year 2006 , my awareness became so strong, connections became so clear to me, I had to now accept my life purpose in helping others.

I give my thanks to the Divine and Angels for the information and photographs I have to now pass on to you to share, as it was they who allowed me to have this experience and they still do.

ENJOY

Index

About Angels

I have been guided to this stage in my life by the Angels and Archangels, I have to pass what knowledge and experiences I have learned to you.

My book includes my own personal photograph's of Angels,

Pure angelic beings, energies, colours and different kinds of orbs, they have all been taken between June 2007 to the present.

I seem to be able to take photograph's and pick up what may be there, the photograph's vary as you will see, my camera is a Samsung SHD digital 8.2pixel, the one before that was the same make but a lower pixel, just ordinary digital cameras.

Some are taken very late at night or early in the morning, the day's were always clear and at night, my garden would be totally pitch black, there are no street lamps around the back garden, any are a fair number of yards away, some were taken on night mode some were not. Some were also taken inside my home, some do have real people in them mainly family members.

They are real photographs, never tampered with, you have my word.

Angel's have always been here and being seen more so

now helping to bring back Peace, Love, and Light to the universe , the Divine intervention to create a better future, find your own inner self or spiritual path.

This may be a long process but change is happening.

I realise many people who have had or thought they had Angel experiences will feel alone, or a little out of place or had no one to talk to about your experiences, I know I did.

Times were confusing and so were experiences.

Another reason I have been guided to write this book is to help bring people together and let you know you are not alone.

Myself I thought … Who will believe me …

About Angels (continued)

There is a lady called Ada Donaldson a Brilliant medium who started Angels Gateway Spiritual Church in Midlothian, Scotland, who use what building they can as they have no permanent residence as yet, a very down to earth lady, that I was able to talk to eventually, once I had the courage, she helped me see more clearly to understand some of my experiences and I thank her.

One thing for sure since I've progressed these last couple of years through Angel guidance and teaching.

I can honestly say Angels are Real.

As well as your spiritual experience, notice how animals wild or tame and children come nearer to you, children stare and smile at you as you pass them by even babies, this may sometimes happen but it is not always the case.

It's as if they can see what we can't.

It is hard to walk with a calmness and peaceful feeling all the time because of the Buzz of life, outside influences, difficulties, problems and the need to achieve your daily routine.

BUT HEY !!!   We are only human and Angels never hold anything against you.

Their Love and Guidance is Unconditional.

As some people may have experienced, Angel's can become human form, especially in times of real need of help for those who have had a near death experience as in a car crash.

There may be someone who suddenly appears and helps you to safety but then they are gone as quick as they arrived.

This does happen, and that is why most refer this experience to their Guardian Angel taking care of them.

But the Angel's will only step in without asking at times when it is an urgent situation and not your time to leave the earth.

We cannot see Angels in their energy form with the human eye because it would blind us, it is as bright as the sun as you will see in some of the photograph's.

About Angels (continued)

One tip the Angels gave me to help progress was to, listen to others, take note of suggestions given, listen to your inner instinct or maybe something you read.

Write them down, this may give you various helpful suggestions or answers for future use, as well as your inner instinct being correct.

Angel's and Archangels are servers, they are only too delighted to be asked for help or guidance anytime day or night.

But they will only oblige if asked by you first.

Talk to your Angels on a daily basis and ask for guidance, talk from the heart and say what you feel or need help with.

I found the "fifteen Archangel oracle cards" by Doreen Virtue helpful, they to gave me courage, confidence and the push to do what I do now, but again this may not be the case for us all.

Actually I didn't just go out and buy the Oracle cards, because I always thought no to cards, probably because I didn't really understand the differences of various types of guidance cards.

One night I was surfing the internet and looking at different types of Angel cards but thought to myself, which ones do you buy ?

I didn't buy any and left it that night, but the next morning when I woke up.

As clear as words could be I was told to buy the fifteen Archangel oracle cards, so I did and have not looked back since.

In the Beginning

My first recollection of a Spiritual experience would have been when I was around seven or eight years old.

I was being welcomed into the Salvation Army Sunday School, (my gran, my dad's mum loved the Salvation Army and her favourite songs were ('The Old Ragged cross and Amazing Grace') anyway I remember kneeling at an altar with two other children, then I remember slightly opening my eyes and what I saw was a huge beam of white light shining down upon me from the skylight.

I never thought anymore of it, as it meant nothing to me.

I did go to Sunday school for a few years and did enjoy the Salvation Army especially when we would get presented with books on special gift day's for our achievements.

When I was around twelve or thirteen years old I was sitting in my bedroom that I shared with my other two sisters, I was looking in the mirror at the time and saw Jesus Christ standing behind me smiling. I turned and looked at him, he was tall, his hair was down to his neck, he had a beard around his chin and face. He wore a long brilliant white gown which reached the floor, the sleeves were the length of his arms and continued downwards to touch the floor. His arms were held out towards me ,there was such kindness coming from his face, the love that flowed was overwhelming. He wore no shoes, his feet were bare. As I turned back to my mirror I still saw him, but as I turned back to look at him again he was gone.

He had not said a word, I believe he was a real person trying to show people a good way of life through Love, Peace and Light.

I never knew what this experience may mean, until one day I told my grandma (my mum's mum), she reckoned it was some sort of calling from the Divine. I did not know what to think. My gran was the only person I told about this until many years later.

In the Beginning (continued)

While I was young I experienced premonitions and visions but I never ever understood these, and sometimes I did not like it because it could feel a little scary.

I tried to block my mind for many years, but this did not stop some experiences as you will read in the next chapter.

I have always' believed in Angels ever since I was small and I can say that I have experienced their presence on numerous occasions.

One thing I have to state is that I was a rather sceptical person regarding Spiritual experiences, but that has changed due to personal experiences and a better understanding of them.

Myself I have the yearning for the truth and my inner intuition is very clear at making me aware when the truth has not been told, to myself that is. Whenever I have been wronged by someone, I have always' given the benefit of the doubt, but even this can only go so far, as the time comes when enough is enough and time to let go. I usually only see the good in people until proven otherwise, which can come as a shock at times and often too late down the line, because damage and pain has already been experienced.

I never seem to think about death as I feel it comes to us all at some point and is part of the universal process of life.

However I do yearn to pass on the Peace, Love and Light of the universe to others as I am guided to.

In the Beginning (continued)

I do believe there is a change occurring universaly in the energies but this is for the good of mankind and the future of the world, us, our children our children's children, I am sure you will agree that a better safer loving world would benefit all.

Angels are becoming more obvious to people as the truth is They Do Exist.

They will help in whatever you may ask them, but you must be open to understanding that answers can come in many forms.

It could be something someone say's, something you read, words that may stand out to you, a sudden change in plans, in your dreams.

Sometimes you may have the feeling to sleep, just sleep this is normal, this may be the way the angels are trying to communicate your answers as you can be more receptive when you are relaxed and asleep.

For me as well as the above, the bottom of my spine often aches as does the top of my crown chakra, sometimes my whole body feels like it is aching, swollen and heavy as if going through some sort of change. This is normal for some but not us all.

But the answer will come when you are ready to grasp it so don't worry about it.

I do not claim to fully understand my experiences because I don't, but I am sure that in time they will become clearer to me with Angel guidance and any advice given from other people.

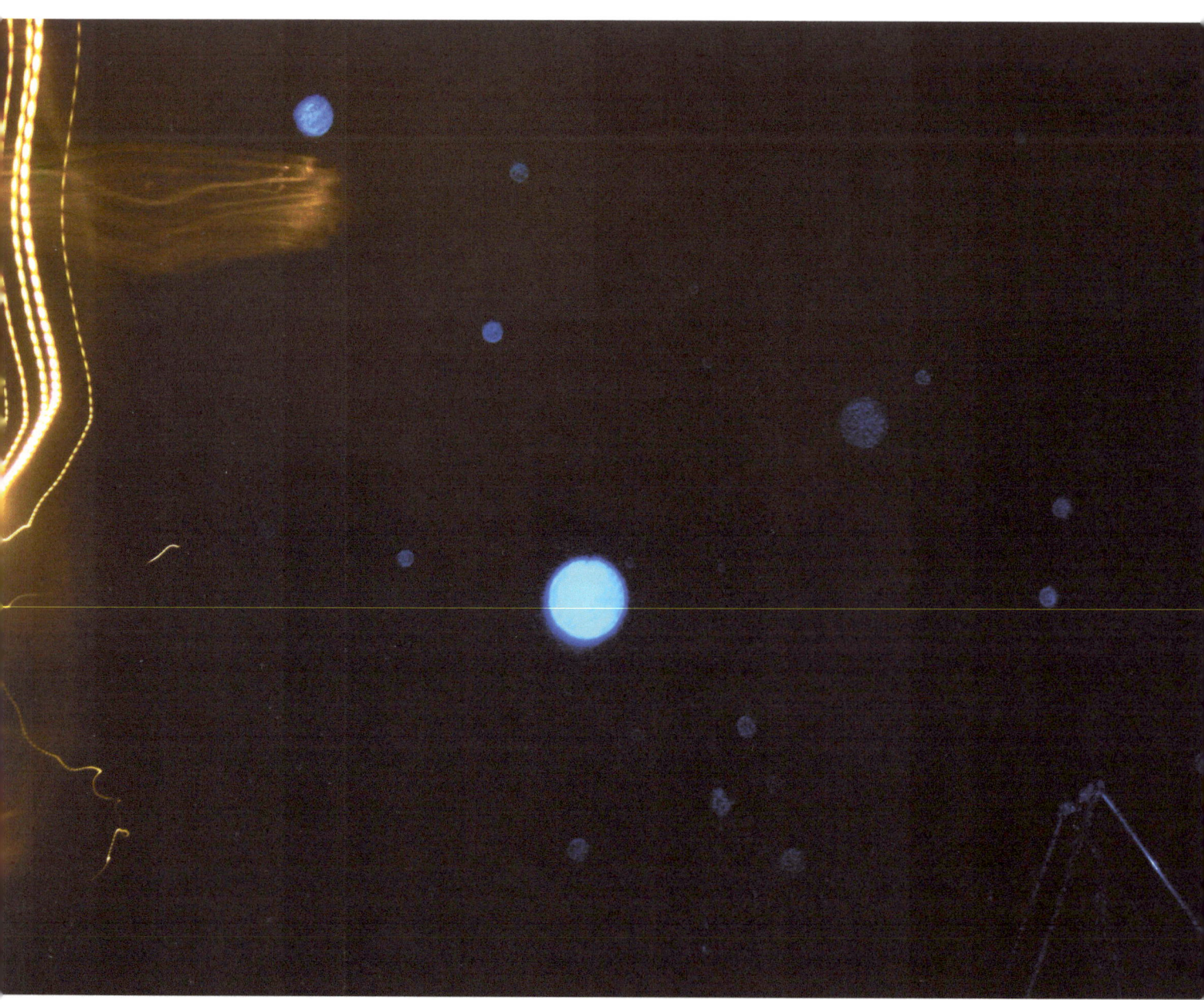

21

True Experiences

I feel I have been given a special gift, as well as clairaudience, claircognizance , clairvoyance and healing I seem to be able to photograph different kinds of beings or energies, I mean Angels, peoples spirits, Orbs, energy, different colours of energy and shapes. I am a healer with people and animals, each persons experience is different and sometimes I use crystals and stones in the healing if guided to or ones that I know help a specific ailment.

My clairvoyance and other aspects mean I hear and receive guidance through Divine / Spiritual experience as well as sensing a presence or picking up smells. Its not like someone talking in your ear, it is more like words, sentences, or even a paragraph will come fleeting into your mind and are repetitive, even pictures if it happens to be a picture. Sometimes the urge to write several pages can happen.

Being peaceful and calm helps this mature, because you cannot predict when a message is coming, it just happens.

Sometimes you may get an inner instinct to change direction, cross the road, say no to something or question a subject or whatever the situation may be. Your inner intuition is usually correct.

My photograph's may shock or leave you confused, but I can assure anyone the time approaching is a peaceful time.

There is too much Greed, Violence, Conflict and Corruption in the world and this must change.

Time for a rethink to our future.

Personally I have had to experience each of these situations, more than once, especially corruption in others.

There are situations I still need to change but it will take a long time. Thrown into financial turmoil, affecting ones health which many people experience , due to the cost of living, no affordable housing and others who do get away with their family responsibilities.

But I am still in a better position than many in the world.

I have water where some do not, I have a roof over my head where some do not.

We have to be thankful for the basics of living never mind the high life, that's a luxury and usually way beyond affordable.

These experiences are difficult and I'd say the hardest part of your inner Spiritual path.

Because you have to learn to let go of the Past, Forgive those who have wronged you and maybe your family, let go of your

anger and upset, as this causes emotional blockage.

We cannot change others or their actions that is up to them, but we can help ourselves.

Ask your Angel to help you release these emotions, crying is good for clearing and very normal, this I know.

Your outlook may be bleak at this moment, but in time you will do great by yourself. Have Courage…

The Respect for human beings to each other is at an all time low.

Each one of you has the ability to make a change for the better.

Angel's have been around thousands and thousands of year's way B.C., way before many idea's were introduced and caused conflict, this was never needed and was not required, the whole human race was meant to be a loving, peaceful race, progress is good but not all and especially when it conflicts with the human race as a whole, we are all equal.

It would be good if everyone could treat their neighbour or anyone else for that matter in the way they would like to be treated themselves.

Change will not happen over night but a little at a time goes a long way.

True Experiences (continued)

My dad in 1977 lost his life in the ambulance on the way to the hospital, he was a mining supervisor and as my dad checked out a mine for the men to work in it collapsed in on him damaging his whole body badly. As the hospital got near my dad was resuscitated and breathing again, he had come back to life although his life was never ever going to be the same again.

I remember the police coming to our door quite late at night and me thinking "what had ones of us done wrong" but we had not done anything.

My mum was so upset and then we all were.

I believe my dad was looked after by Angels and helped to survive, though I was only young I constantly asked for help for my dad even though I had little understanding of the spiritual realm at that time.

He is now in his 65th year and although still very disabled, tries so hard to get on with daily life, it is far from easy but he does very well.

My mum had a hard time bringing four of us up as well as caring for my dad and deserves a big round of applause from all her family.

Without my parents I would not have got through many situations over the years on my own and I thank them.

Love & Light & Angel Blessings to you mum and dad, my brother Douglas and my two sisters Catherine and Helena and their families.

True Experiences (continued)

My parents allowed me to have a horse when I was sixteen years old as long as I worked and paid for its upkeep myself, I did.

I bought him when he was three years old, he was a chestnut cross arab / thoroughbred, he had a white blaze down his face and three white socks. I called him Sonney.

He became my best friend and companion, horses were my first love. We used to do little competitions, show jumping, gymkhana's and cross country events.

Until one day he started to become ill, he was only five years old, he started to not be able to walk properly this affected his whole health and he was in lots of pain. I had him at the vets numerous times and he had many different painkillers, but he was now being bullied in the field by the other horses because he could not fight back. I had to stable him next.

A test later showed he had brucelosis a disease which affected his bones while growing, it was incurable and the only kind thing I could do for him would be to put him to sleep, I hated that thought but knew I had to for his sake.

The day I had to walk him from the field to the stables and then go to the animal hospital I can never forget. He totally leaned on me to support him walking and all I could do was cuddle him.

It was as if he knew what was coming next, my mum and I followed the horse box to the animal hospital, Sonney kept looking around at us, all I could do was cry.

Sonney will never be forgotten and the reason why I include this story is that I am sure it is now his spirit which lives with me, and he has also shown himself in a photograph which is printed in this book. He has been well cared for and is well, animals and all natural given gifts are cared for also by Angels.

True Experiences (continued)

Over the years I have had many knocks to my life in more way's than one, from divorce to health issues, but I have always' asked for help and guidance when I remembered to and do feel I have been helped, even though it may not have felt like it at the time.

Myself I have been very much a christian follower for years, but my spiritual experiences started opening my eyes to see a bigger universal picture, for the better. It also made me very much more openminded to many subjects and to accept so many as in the "Law of one", we are all the same.

I remember when I had only worked for a year or so, I had a route I would follow day in day out to and from work. But one day I took a detour for no real reason and went in another direction, I did not go through the back of the shops as normal at lunchtime.

I later discovered that a serious incident had taken place at the bank at the time I would have walked passed it, the incident involved guns.

I am sure I was guided by Angels that day to take a different path.

True Experiences (continued)

In the year 2002 our home back then had just been fitted with a carbon monoxide detector. The next day the alarm went off at around 6pm, it would not stop and we could not turn it off.

I called the gas people this was now classed as an emergency and they had to come out within an hour, they did.

Carbon monoxide was detected from the fire so the whole gas system had to be shut down and condemned until it was replaced.

You cannot smell or see carbon monoxide and it is deadly.

Myself and my family were in the house, if we had all gone to bed and the detector had not been fitted the day before we may not have been here today.

Even though experiences I have already written are just a few, there were many more in the past and more to come.

In the year 2006 my family and I had to move house, we moved to a country cottage it is lovely, very gothic looking and over two hundred years old, it was like a dream come true.

Actually I did not think I would get the cottage but we did and I was so pleased. Myself and my three children settled although it did take a little time, we got there though. We did not like all the creepy crawlies but learned to share.

True Experiences (continued)

I am one not for doing much at Halloween but this Halloween in 2007 I decided to throw a party, so I did.

Many friends came with their children and my families came, it was great fun, we were all dressed up it was a blast.

This was when spiritual orbs really started to show in photographs I took, even though there were a few in photo's in the summerhouse I had had built in the garden.

I was gob smacked at these photo's but started to become more aware of spiritual presences in the house.

Some experiences were a little startling but we got used to it.

In November 2007 I invited mediums and psychics to the house to see if they could help with the houses history and goings on.

I myself found out some history of the house before the mediums came, I also must point out that I was not fully aware of myself being clairvoyant yet.

There were nine people turned up the night of the vigil at the house, we were all excited. They split into two groups I joined one and my sister and mum joined the other.

The outcome was that there are several spirits with the house, all for their own personal reasons and each different circumstances.

Some were related to when they worked here back in the 17th/18th century, some were when this land was used by the forces in World War 2 and some just lived and died here at some point. So it was their home long before ours. That night help confirm a few suspicions that I knew by finding out some of the houses history, at least experiences were not of the imagination. I must add the house spirits are nothing to do with the Angel energies and photo's they are different.

True Experiences (continued)

In June 2007 I had a Victorian style summerhouse built, I filled it with different chimes, shapes, crystals and candles, I loved it it was a chill room. Somewhere to go for a bit of peace and quiet.

I mention the summerhouse because you will see it in some of the photograph's I have printed in the book. At times it always looked lit up inside in photo's but there was nothing on inside the summerhouse at all.

The photograph's are mainly all taken by me and are originals, apart from some changes in light in some they are what they show, some were taken on night mode some on normal. The colours are real and so are shapes, my back garden is usually pitch black there are no street lamps around the garden and any are a number of yards away. The cottage sits on its own and not near another house.

Something I should point out is that other people with different camera's have taken photo's at my home, but did not come out with ones like I have captured except orbs and some light shapes. The photograph's were all taken on different day's, times, months and usually with different people in them. They were always' taken on clear night's, day's and morning's whether dark or light, some were also taken indoors.

True Experiences (continued)

Another time I had an unpleasant experience in a home we used to live in.

One night when I was sleeping I woke to get up to go to the bathroom, but found I could not move, something or someone was pressing on my chest so I could not get up, there was noone to see. I just closed my eyes and kept asking for help from the Divine to save me, the experience eventually subsided although I was left shaken and a little scared.

I do believe there are two sides to everything.

Do not dismiss unhealthy energies as non existant because they do.

In the year 2000 I developed a rare exzema on my hands and feet, it was like blisters that just keep eating the skin, blistering over and over and does not let the skin heal, I was given a special cream to help keep it supple and I had to wear cotton gloves and socks constantly.

By spring 2001 it had all gone, how I do not know. Now and again I can still see little blisters on my hands under the skin but it does not come to anything.

In May 2001 I bought a pajero 4x4 from someone down south, I had to go half way and pick it up at Scotch corner in England to bring it back up to the lothians where I live, possibly a hundred and sixty miles.

A few day's after I had it at home I needed to book it into the local garage as it was not driving properly.

It turned out that there was no cam belt and the timing belt was in shreds, that pajero should never have got me home safe at all or drive when I reached home.

All I can say is I am so grateful to the Angels for looking after me.

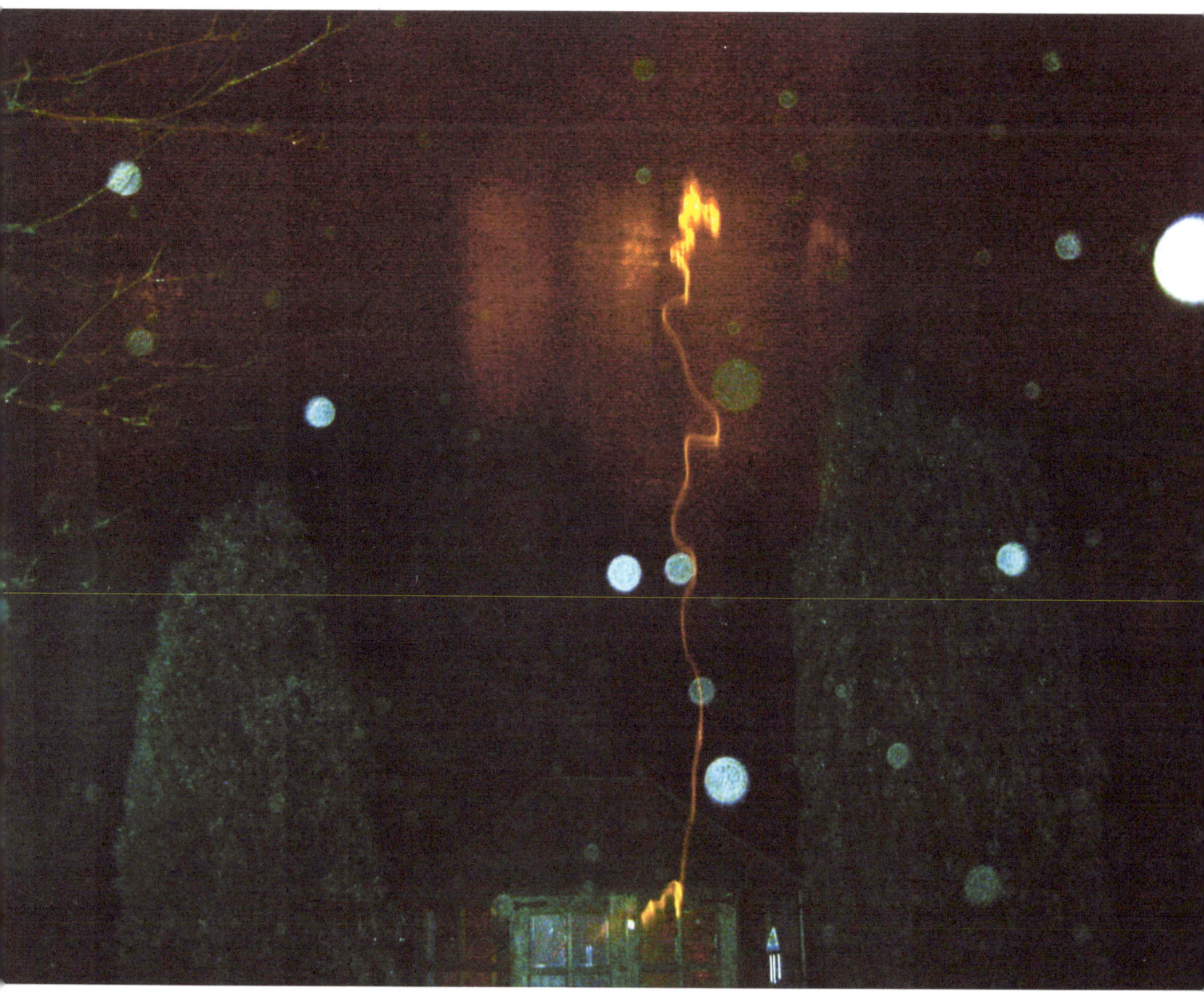

Meditation Experiences

My first real meditation experience took place in January 2008, I had not really thought about doing it before, as all these years I just used to lie down, close my eyes, regulate my breathing and often think about being in a warm sunny place. Lovely.

Now I will light a candle, make myself comfortable either sitting or lying down, then I will get my breathing regulated and feel in a state of total relaxation.

I will then ask the Angels if there is any guidance they can give me or are there any messages for me to have, a meditation can last up to an hour pending on yourself of course.

Each meditation can be very different, in some you may see in your minds eye pictures, people, words anything really, and other times your meditation may be just full of swirling colours or a bright white light.

The best thing to do is write it down after each meditation, as it is also an experience to look back on and read it over again and again, to refresh your memory and realise you did experience this.

In January 2008, I lit a candle and asked Archangel Michael for protection and guidance, which you can do.

I closed my eyes and I automatically saw a dark blue door closed, but beaming bright light was seeping out from all around the edges of the door.

I asked the Angels for guidance and to show me what I was experiencing meant and what was my purpose. I was disturbed so woke up, I now had to stop the meditation, the blue door stayed closed.

Meditation Experiences (continued)

January 2008, I was changing the sheets on my bed, I lay on it for a few moments and spoke to the Angels.

My mind stayed blank but a huge feeling of love, peace and forgiveness came over me, so much so that I had tears rolling down my cheeks, I was overwhelmed.

My eyes were still closed there then was a bright light in the distance, it came no further. Then I saw a beautiful female angel standing alone with her wings partly up, she then disappeared.

It was as if she was waiting for someone.

I opened my eyes said thank you and got up.

It left me feeling that all my hurt, pain, sadness had now left me, but my stomach felt like I had butterflies in it.

I must state this experience was not a meditation.

Still January 2008

I woke up in the early hours as I was asleep in bed, I do not know what time it was, but there was something at one of my bedroom window's, my bedroom is on the ground floor.

Still half asleep I looked at my window, there was a pure white light shining through my blind as bright as the sun.

I did not get up to open the blind, and I was not afraid.

It was so bright it lit up my whole bedroom as if a light was on except brighter.

My first thought was "what", and then I went back to sleep.

Meditation Experiences (continued)

January 2008

This time I did meditate, my head was mainly full of swirling colours like going through a tunnel, the colours were pink, blue, green, orange, white.

On this night my cat began to act strange, he kept wandering around the house meowing, he then came up to me, I was lying on the settee and he meowed and meowed.

He then jumped up on me and snuggled in to sleep.

My cat never does this and he is not a cuddly cat he even crept nearer to my arms.

I believe he was sensing the Angel energy in the room that night and knew to come to me for comfort.

February 2008

I lit a red candle today and lay down to meditate.

I asked the Angels to show me how to progress in my spiritual journey. My head was full of spirals, waves and circles of many colours and at times would go brilliant white.

My body would feel heavy and light at times, there was also a tingling feeling travelling from my feet upwards.

The bottom of my spine ached.

At times I could partially see faces at a distance in my mind although they were not clear. A lady approached me quite clearly, she was tall, had a furry hat and like an eye mask over her eyes, she was very slim and elegant looking, her dress was green. She did not speak. I was disturbed so had to end the meditation, the white light was present at times in my meditation also.

Meditation Experiences (continued)

March 2008

I saw a very old man in a white robe, his hair and beard were very long and pure white, he was just standing in front of me, looking right at me.

Then a pure white unicorn came charging towards me from his left hand side, it then disappeared.

I then saw a man in coloured clothing, sort of a tunic but made with very fine cloth and thread, it was navy blue with gold patterns on it and gold edging.

He had blonde hair and a pale face.

Then colours appeared and just kept moving downwards and swirling.

I saw a man but he was so high up in the clouds and sky, the colours were now golden and white.

I cannot give detail of the man because he was so high up in the sky, but I felt like I was rising up towards him, it was like I was being pulled up from the stomach.

Then I just remember closing with Angel wings in front of my eyes, it was an Angel standing with its back to me.

Two messages I was given.

1/ not to be afraid of others and their thoughts.

2/ everything will become alright.

Meditation Experiences (continued)

March 2008

I went to bed at eleven pm, I put my light off and my room seemed to stay darker than normal.

I could hear one bird outside cooing away and another chirping non stop.

My bedroom window became a very red/orange colour but this was on the outside, it stayed there for about a minute and then went away, I am not sure what that presence may have been.

My room then went back to normal, I had actually sat up put my glasses on and watched the window. It was amazing.

The birds stopped making noises after the colour had left my window.

March 2008

I got myself ready for a meditation.

I remember swirls of colours, like going through a tunnel, there were gold, blue, white, pink, green,

There were flashes of faces looking at me, I did not know these faces and they passed so quickly that I could not describe them.

There was an angel in the distance, but I did not see her clearly, the surrounding's were white and golden.

Meditation Experiences (continued)

April 2008

I put my head in my hands on top of my dining table, as I closed my eyes there was a very tall male Angel standing in front of me, he was wearing metal armour, he had blonde hair but I could not make out his face.

It was body armour he wore, short armoured pleated skirt, ankle type metal armour and held a huge sword in his hand, I mean huge, because as he held it in his hand the point actually touched the ground.

He did not speak, only stayed standing in front of me, then I awoke and he was gone.

April 2008

I lay down to do a meditation, as I closed my eyes my mind went black and dark, the swirls of colours were more brown, whites and black then it began to clear into pure white.

Sitting on a throne looking at me, was an older man with pure white long hair, pure white long beard and a pure white long robe, similar to a man I had saw before.

He stood up looked at me, turned his back and then he was gone.

His face was oriental and tanned as were his hands tanned.

Then my mind became a swirl of colours again except they were white, pale pinks, dark pinks, lilac, deep purple, then unfortunatly I was disturbed so ended my meditation.

Meditation Experiences (continued)

May 2008

I closed my eyes at around 10am, this was not a meditation.

I saw an Angel but he was so tall I could not see his face or shoulder's they were miles and miles up into the sky and clouds.

He was so like a giant robot, I could see the ending's of his wings only, which were a brown colour on the inside, his legs had like silver metallic covering and he wore silver ankle boots.

I awoke.

June 2008

In my meditation today I saw in the distance a golden lion surrounded in a deep summer green colour, almost like a backing colour in a picture as it was all around the lion.

Then I got flashes of faces and pictures but I could not tell what they were as they passed so quickly.

Then my head filled with colours, white, pink, lilac, green.

I then brought myself back to awaken.

July 2008

I sat down in a chair at around 9.30am, closed my eyes and relaxed. I felt I was surrounded by a presence as there was a slight coldness all around my body, but I felt safe, it was like a protection shield.

There were strange energy feeling's going through my body and I felt as if my whole body was pure white within, like being washed down from head to toe in pure white light, it had a cleansing feeling but felt very powerful. This lasted about half an hour and I did feel slightly off balance for a few moments afterwards.

Meditation Experiences (continued)

August 2008

I had been awake since 4.30am for some reason, so I got up.

About half an hour later I lay down on my settee, I saw many colours, pink, gold, red, white, the sun shone in on me and was warm.

I saw numerous faces of lions and briefly a woman's face, I kept being told " have courage".

August 2008

Today I did a chakra alignment with the cd I have.

This was totally amazing, my mind and body were a constant flow of colours.

Pink, purple, white, gold, orange, blue, yellow.

I briefly got disturbed but returned to complete the exercise.

I saw an Indian lady with clasped hands raising them up into the air.

There was also a presence with me as I could feel the slight coldness all around me, like wearing a cape even with the hood up.

It felt like my mind was being worked on .

This experience was total mind blowing, it felt as if the presence was actually me, within me, a strange feeling but not frightening at all it was almost natural.

At the end I saw a pure white unicorn standing in front of me, then I awoke.

49

How I Was Guided to Healing

If I think back a number of years, I always had this thought that I wished I could take peoples pain away, and this thought often crept into my head at times, I'm not sure why.

When my children were ill I would have them sleep beside me hoping that I would contract their illness from them, to make them well.

This sometimes worked, I think.

Becoming aware of my healing hands became more apparant from around the middle of 2007.

My hands would become hot for no reason or so I thought in the beginning.

Then as my guidance from the Angels became stronger and I finally accepted my life purpose, some thoughts started to fit into place and make sense.

The first time I put my hands on someone to heal was my mums sore knees. The heat became very intense from my hands and since then practice and guidance have brought me to almost perfection.

I was guided and shown by the Angels how to work a healing as I learned something new each time I did one.

It is as if they would correct me.

My hands will now go hot in presences of people as if letting me know that someone near needs healing or help.

Even just standing by a friend my hands may become intensly

Hot as if a healing is needed.

But one thing is you cannot just send out a healing or give it, it must be asked for or you have been given permission to proceed.

This is something I have been guided to know.

Healing hands is an amazing gift and I am privileged to be able to do this for people and animals.

I thoroughly enjoy helping others it is something that is close to me heart.

Connecting to your Angels

Take some quiet time for yourself, I know from personal experience that this can be difficult for some, so don't be hard on yourself every little helps.

Or a good time also is before you close your eyes at night in bed. I do this myself.

You have to ask an angel for help, they cannot connect to you otherwise, they cannot intrude without being asked first.

If you have never asked your Guardian Angel or any Angel to come near and give you help before, all you need to do is ask them to come into your life.

You may feel a warm glow come over you, or a tingling feeling or a slight coldness by your side, or maybe even nothing at all to begin with as they will not do anything if you are not ready, so as not to alarm you.

Sometimes you may see small flashes of white light pass the corner of your eyes, this can mean an Angel is near.

Do not fear or worry as this is all very normal, then talk to them as if they were standing or sitting beside you, because they are.

All you need to say is Angel's I need your help or guidance, and they will be near you listening.

Answers:- These can come in many forms, it could be what someone say's, something you read, words that may stand out to you, an intuition feeling, even dreams pictures and repetative words that may come into you mind.

The sudden urge to write something down, do so.

Go with what feels right for you.

Connecting to your Angels (continued)

Learn to meditate, there is no specific type of meditation for Angels, just relax regulate your breathing, burn a candle to show you are walking in the light, some light music and just talk, or while walking or sitting in natural surroundings, as in the countryside talk to your angels openly.

Don't worry too much about the kind of music, Angels like what you like, even a good bit of Rock now and again. Yes really.

They love nothing more than, love, laughter, happiness, parties, and the birth of a new born baby.

You do not need to meditate to bring an Angel to you just talk, talk from the heart.

If you are looking for a specific Angel for a specific difficulty or problem, then read through the information I have researched and gathered together, to make it simplistic for people to understand on the fifteen Archangels that may be able to help you best.

I also feel that the fifteen Archangels are the most powerful beings to help mankind, and that I was guided to those specific Angels and information. I do believe there are many many more we do not yet know much about.

All you have to do is call their name and they will listen to you, just talk.

Again answers can come in many forms as with the other Angels, and it does not always come as quick as you would like it to or sometimes make sense at the time.

But be reassured the timing or form of your answer comes when it is the correct time for you to grasp it.

Connecting to your Angels (continued)

Patience is needed, this even I had to learn to appreciate as I am not always the most patient of people.

Something else that may help you in your quest is, being near water whether the sea, lake, river, the swimming pool, a bath or shower even. Can be very cleansing, relaxing and put you in touch with your inner self. (a bubble lamp even helps).

The same applies to being in Nature, whether walking in the woods, being in the fresh air or admiring the countryside from a distance. Taking note of all the natural surroundings that are taken for granted.

Water and Nature is a part of your Spiritual self being, bringing to you a clearer way of thinking or maybe even answers you seek.

Myself since I was very young always get a yearning to be beside water, either the swimming pool, sea or anywhere really.

I love doing them all when possible and I have learned to appreciate nature and water more so.

If I have not been near water or nature for a while I do get an almighty nudge to make time for it.

Spiritualy the experience for anyone is so uplifting, calming and clearing, you will benefit from doing any of these at times.

Going forward with your Angels by your side is a personal experience and individual, but do not give up.

Your ability will come from within and become easier for you to understand as time goes by.

If you feel uncomfortable at anytime, challenge who is present and ask as much as you like, until you feel comfortable.

Connecting to your Angels (continued)

I should mention that clutter around the home can cause blockages, whether it be clothes lying around, cleaning needing done, or just too much belongings.

The residue from emotions causes blockage even if they have lingered for years and years, even from people who have already passed away into the spirit world.

Plenty of fresh air through the home helps clear this, as does burning incense sticks, or asking Archangel Michael to clear away lower energies.

Cleansing your home as you would cleanse yourself of psychic residue mentally and bodily, its good for the home to be done every now and again to.

An Angel never goes by their name and do not tell you what to do.

Remember their Love and Guidance is Unconditional no matter who YOU are or where you are.

An Angel loves nothing more than helping, consoling and guiding us human beings.

Only sometimes just say Thankyou that is all.

LOVE & LIGHT

The Fifteen Archangels

ARCHANGEL   MICHAEL

ARCHANGEL   GABRIEL

ARCHANGEL   RAPHAEL

ARCHANGEL   HANIEL

ARCHANGEL   JEREMIEL

ARCHANGEL   CHAMUEL

ARCHANGEL   URIEL

ARCHANGEL   METATRON

ARCHANGEL   ZADKIEL

ARCHANGEL   RAGUEL

ARCHANGEL   RAZIEL

ARCHANGEL   JOPHIEL

ARCHANGEL   AZRAEL

ARCHANGEL   ARIEL

ARCHANGEL   SANDALPHON

The Archangel Individual Uses For Yourself

ARCHANGEL MICHAEL (NAME MEANS- HE WHO IS LIKE GOD/CREATOR)

You can ask him for help with the following :-

Ask him to enter your dreams to clear away any fears that are blocking you from fully enjoying and living your spiritual gifts and qualities.

Ask him to protect you, your loved ones, your home and possessions with powerful loving light.

The light repels your lower energies and attracts loving experiences, focus on the light instead of fear, you are safe at all times.

Worthiness and increased self-esteem, space clearing, motivation, energy and vitality, direction, courage, commitments, dedication to ones beliefs, bring great success to all ventures involving career, work, business, commerce.

His Aura colour is:- Royal Blue mixed with tinges of Purple.
His crystal is :- Sugalite

ARCHANGEL METATRON:(HE WAS HUMAN BEFORE BECOMING AN ANGEL)

He can assist with the following:-

Attention Deficit Disorder (ADD)
Attention Deficit Hyperactivity Disorder (ADHD)
Children issues, Record keeping, Organization, Spiritual Understanding, writing.
Helps clear and align chakra energy centres, as in psychic toxins from your body.
Increased Intuition, and helps with organizing your priorities.

His Aura is :- Violet with sea foam green stripes.
His Crystal is Phenacite or Watermelon tourmaline.\

ARCHANGEL GABRIEL :- (NAME MEANS GOD/CREATOR IS MY STRENGTH)

She can assist you with the following :-

Enhances Intuition, brings inner happiness and peace of mind, guarantees safety in all
    travel.
Art related projects and artists, child conception, fertility, writing, publishing, journalism,
    television and radio work.
Adopting children, interviews, careers.
As you nurture children do not forget your own inner child, you can laugh, be silly, and
    have just as much love inside.

Her Aura colour is :- Pale Blue
Her Crystal is:- Herkiline diamond / Citrine / Copper

Archangel Jeremiel :- (name means Mercy of God/Creator)

He can assist with the following :-

Clairvoyance, prophetic visions, life reviews, making life changes, psychic dreams including their interpretations.
Ask him to help you take stock of your life and use what is important for today and tomorrow.
Ask him to help you be positive in your outlook attracting a loving solution and letting go.

His Aura colour is :- Deep Eggplant Purple
His Crystal is :- Amethyst

Archangel Chamuel :- (name means He who sees God/Creator/ He who seeks God/Creator)

He can assist with the following :-

Finding a Soulmate, relationships building on them and strengthening them.
Offers divine protection from all acts of violence, war terror.
Finding the right career or career path, life purposes, finding lost items, World Peace, centering and calming yourself. Helps clear the old ready for the new.
Hold love in your heart, mind and thoughts, this is the foundation of peace and love.

His Aura colour is :- Pale Green.
His Crystal is :- Green flourite / Ruby crystal

Archangel Raphael :- (name means whom God/Creator heals or has healed)

He can assist with the following :-

Protection for travellers and luggage, weightloss, harmony, spiritual releasement, addictions, and eliminating and reducing cravings, physical and spiritual eyesight, clairvoyance, guidance and support for healers, healing humans and animals, retrieving lost pets, space clearing.
Ask for help in whatever form, he can help calm you.
Financial security and divine protection from all negative forces.
Blessings of good health.

His Aura colour is :- Emerald Green.
His Crystal is :- Emeralds, Pink danburite, Malachite.

Archangel Ariel :- (name means Lioness of God/Creator)

She can assist with the following :-

Protects oceans, lakes, animals, divine magic, manifestations, enviromentalism, brings messages from and delivers messages to the deceased.
Ask her for courage, to stand up for whatever your beliefs may be. Give all your worries to her.

Her Aura colour is :- Pale Pink
Her Crystal is :- Rose quartz

Archangel Zadkiel :- (name means the rightousness of God/Creator)

He can assist with the following :-

Compassion, finding lost objects, forgiveness of self and others, emotional and physical healing, memory enhancement and remembering important things.
To approach situations with a loving heart to allow solutions to come forth.
Ask anything you wish to know.
The gift of wisdom and inner peace.
He can also bring good fortune in all matters involving games of chance, e.g. the lottery.

His Aura colour is :- Deep Indigo Blue
His Mineral is :- Lapis Lazuli / Amethyst clusters

Archangel Raguel :- (name means friend of God/Creator)

He can assist with the following :-

Resolving arguments, co-operation and harmony.
Defending the unfairly treated, empowerment, mediation of disputes, orderliness, divine order.
Ask him to help you keep positive and optimistic and to help speed along resolution quicker.
Ask him to bring peace to a situation and co-operation, love and understanding.

His Aura is :- Pale Blue
His crystal is :- Aquamarine

ARCHANGEL RAZIEL :- (NAME MEANS SECRET OF GOD/CREATOR)

He can assist with the following :-

Alchemy, clairvoyance, divine magic, manifestations, psychic abilities.
Ask him to help you understand ideas that defy normal logic or help you uncover truths and secrets of spiritual understanding.

His Aura is :- All colours of the rainbow.
His Crystal is :- Clear Quartz.

ARCHANGEL JOPHIEL :- (NAME MEANS BEAUTY OF GOD/CREATOR)

She can assist with the following :-

Art related projects and artists, beautiful thoughts, interior decorating, slowing down from a hectic pace to experience peace and grace.
Getting rid of clutter, getting outdoors.
Clear the energy around you and use feng chui.
Ask her to connect you to nature, nature helps you renew your spirit and revives your energy level.

Her Aura is :- Deep Rose Pink
Her crystal is :- Dark pink, Pink Rubellite, Amethyst point.

Archangel Azrael : - (name means Whom God/Creator helps)

He can assist with the following :-

Your loved ones will work with your Guardian Angel to help you be peaceful, dream visits
    or presence felt means know
they are happy and free from all suffering.
Comforting the dying and grieving, crossing over of the newly deceased persons soul.
Grief counselling and grief counsellors.
Supporting the grieving materially, spiritualy and emotionaly.
Ask and he can be with you at your time of need, whether it be hurt, reflection or
    comfort.
Ask him about your departed ones.

His Aura colour is :- Vanilla Cream (pale yellow tone)
His crystal is :- Creamy yellow Calcite / Moldavite

Archangel Sandalphon :- (he was Human before becoming an angel, also known as Elijah)

He can assist with the following :-

Music, delivering and answering prayers, determining the gender of an unborn child,
    integrity, appreciation of miracles and victories.
Releasing fears, can help you speak truth openly in a way that benefits everyone.

His Aura colour is :- Cool shade of Turquiose
His crystal is :- Aventurine (green) / Turquiose stone

ARCHANGEL URIEL :- (NAME MEANS GOD/CREATOR IS LIGHT, GOD/CREATORS LIGHT FIRE OF GOD/CREATOR)

He can assist you with the following :-

Weather, writing and writing projects, students, studying, understanding, solutions to difficulties, divine magic, earth changes, spiritual understanding.
Ask him for all the support you need to bring any ideas to fruitition.

His Aura colour is :- Pale Yellow
His Crystal is :- Amber / Diamond

ARCHANGEL HANIEL :- (NAME MEANS GLORY OR GRACE OF GOD/CREATOR)

She can assist with the following :-

Bringing Grace into our lives, healing, abilities, moon energy, psychic abilities especially clairvoyance.
She will care for you with her nurturing mother energy.
Ask her to guide and nurture you in your direction for happiness and passion. She can bring success in all matters involving love and matters of the heart.
Ask her to assist in natural cycles, moods, rhythms, and all aspects of ourselves, whether feeling unsure or bad about yourself. She will help you see how beautiful you are right now.

Her Aura colour is :- Bluish - white
Her crystal is :- Moonstone / Clear apophylite cluster

Healing

Being able to heal may not come to us all, as this can be an individual and personal experience but worth knowing about.

You cannot give or send a healing unless asked for or given permission first.

You can of course ask an Angel to send help or guidance for someone.

Light a candle a half an hour or more before starting as this helps the energy to collect in the room and shows you are working in the light, it is best that it is a quiet room or area.

You may wish to ask Archangel Michael for protection, this can be done in meditations also. He will surround you with a white protecting light while you work, this helps keep away any unwanted lower energies if present.

You may wish to ask Archangel Raphael for help with the healing you are about to do, he is one of the Archangels who can help with healings.

Being free of toxins may help the energy flow purer, easier and more freely. Toxins as in :- caffeine, smoking, alcohol, being free of toxins at least an hour or more before hand may help.

Toxins can cause blockages in your own system.

Ask the Angels to be present and help with the healing and speak to them before, and after thank them for their help and guidance.

It is best a person is lying down on a therapy table, but healing energy can still help those who cannot lie down, whatever is best for the client concerned.

The heat from your hands can merge from your whole body, this is normal.

Crystals and stones can be used if you feel guided to use them.

Healing (continued)

The heat from your hands may also vary pending on the client, don't worry if you don't feel your hands are hot because the client will.

You may wish to put a light blanket over the client.

Head , hands and feet are like outlets as are other areas such as the mouth, ears and nostrils, letting out lower energies, e.g. pain or emotions.

Your hands are filling the person with pure positive healing energy, helping to balance the body, mind and ailments they may have.

The healing energy works from the inside out and at the core of problems.

Working from right to left and down the body, so as to keep the energy balanced and flowing, start from the head and finish with the head.

Your hands flow over the persons body about two inches above is fine, there is no need for hands on although this can be done if you feel guided to.

A presence may be felt as if working along beside you, you may even feel your hands differently, that there is heat first then a slight coldness in between the heat and your actual hand. This is normal.

This could be help you are receiving to work the healing.

Depending on yourself a healing can last forty to sixty minutes.

Once you have finished your healing a stone such as hematite can be used by the client as a grounding stone, they gently rub it between their hands.

You must also give yourself fifteen to twenty minutes to yourself with a cup of tea or a cold drink, before starting another healing.

Healing (continued)

Each clients experience will be different but sometimes there are similarities, e.g. a presence being felt or floating in air, tingles and just total relaxation.

Two points I clearly notice when I know a client is totally relaxed is :- there feet and toes wiggle and the strain and stress in their face changes to complete relaxation and a look of peacefulness and calm.

Practice makes perfect, I really had to learn this and persevere, the more you can practice the better you will become at perfecting your own technique, finding out what works best for you and your clients.

Each of us may be slightly different in our work, but do what you feel guided to do.

Even before starting a healing it is best to cleanse the room you use, whether it be opening the window's for a bit, hoovering, sweeping, burning insence sticks as well as asking Archangel Michael to clear any lower energies present from the room.

This makes the room feel purer, fresher and ready for new energy being used, also its preventing blockages in you, meaning the energy flow's free easily while you work with it.

LOVE & LIGHT

Recommended Authors

Actually I have not read that many books, most of my experiences and guidance came from being taught by the Angels themselves.

I thank the Divine and the Angels with all my heart for the experiences brought to me that I want to now pass on to you.

There are three authors that I found useful and helpful and maybe you will to.

Doreen Virtue, she is author of many Angel books and cards.

Diana Cooper, she also is author to many books on varies elementals, Angels and Orbs.

Richard Webster, his four books on the Archangels, Michael, Raphael, Gabriel and Uriel are very interesting to read.

But you use what is good for you.

THE LAW OF ONE"

In a book by Diana Cooper you will read what she has regarding the law of one and many other spiritual guidance, it is a very helpful book indeed.

The book is called " A little light on the Spiritual law's"

The law of one mainly means that everyone is equal no one is different , we are all the same.

From colour to beliefs to animals, to sexuality.

We are all the same.

I believe this to be true for everyone.

LOVE & LIGHT

A Little Note

IN THE ARMS OF THE ANGEL

YOU WILL ALWAYS FEEL SAFE

LET YOUR THOUGHTS OF THE

WORLD AND ALL YOUR

TROUBLES

SUBSIDE FOR A FEW MOMENTS

AND ASK FOR PEACE & GUIDANCE

written by Susan Cormack

Descriptions for the photograph's

Page 7:- Looking towards the top of the trees there are six images, four are whitish blue, one is clearly red and the other a paler shaped red to the front.

Page 8:- October 2007, we had a Halloween party and all these orbs came to join in the fun.

Page 9:- Angelic energy with orbs present and there are lots of tiny white specks of light to.

Page 10:- To the right of the summerhouse there is a huge amount of Angelic energy, a face can be seen in this and lots of tiny specks of white light around on the ground.

Page 11:- Front side of the house, white line of light dancing around and a huge amount of angelic energy, how it became this colour I do not know, it is pretty dark in that area.

Page 12:- Lots of angelic energy around in the back garden and many white specks of light.

Page 16:- My daughter holding my niece, the baby was crying, angelic energy lifted the image of the teddy sitting beside them to give to the baby.

Page 17:- I had been doing written work and I asked if it could be blessed, in the right corner of the photo there is an Angel figure and a lot of angelic energy around.

Descriptions for the Photograph's (continued)

Page 18:- The back garden, above the summerhouse there is lots of angelic energy, to the left of this picture a ladies face and long hair can be seen.

Page 19:- New Year 2008 just after midnight in the back garden, dancing lights appearing, and a angelic being looking attached to my mum. Is this a Healing Angel ?

Page 20:- Lots of dancing lights appearing as well as orbs, I think the angelic energy uses anything electrical if on to make shapes appear, as I did have Christmas lights up but they are not in this picture. My daughters face can be seen very faintly at the bottom of this picture, she is standing on top of the trampoline.

Page 21:- Me in the snow in daytime, some orbs can be seen as well as the falling snow.

Page 22:- The back garden, taken on night mode this red coloured energy appeared.

Page 27:- My birthday June 2008, this is what happened in one of my photo's, there are two real people in this photo. But you can clearly see a horse rearing on its hind legs and what looks like lots of streamers being thrown. Amazing.

Page 33:- Daytime, lots of orbs can be seen as well as tiny white specks of light.

Page 34:- The trees at the bottom of the garden, this sort of pink/purple and blue colour appeared.

Descriptions for the Photograph's (continued)

Page 35:- A huge orb present at the bottom of the garden, this was around 7.15am, one or two other orbs can also be seen. I do actually have more photo's of this orb because it moved from my far left to be round in this position.

Page 36:- Daytime, as well as some small orbs and tiny specks of white light, there is to the right of this photo an Angel holding a baby.

Page 37:- The summerhouse, Angelic energy surrounding it with many orbs present.

Page 38:- New Year 2008, not long after midnight, the angelic energy has used the street lamps which are many yards away from the garden to make the lights dance. Myself, my youngest son and my nephew are standing by the rowan tree, my hand is on the rowan tree, but myself and my son look very transparent why? I don't know. Several orbs are around.

Page 39:- My living room, the walls are actually lilac but the energy has changed it to blue and pink, where the white line has come from I've no idea. I must point out that most times when photographs were taken all electrical items were switched off, except a small lamp which sits in a corner.\

Page 40:- The summerhouse at the bottom of the garden, there are no lights on in the summerhouse and it looks as if it has been elevated into the sky, there are also many orbs around.

Page 49:- A sea of orbs, where the colour and the lights came from I do not know.

Descriptions for the Photograph's (continued)

Page 50:- The summerhouse, dancing lights, many specks of white light, red energy around, orbs and to the right of this photo an Angel is standing at the fence.

Page 51:- The back of the house, lots of angelic energy around and many tiny specks of light.

Page 52:- My nephew in the back garden at the halloween party, many orbs are around, the red light to the right I think was a street lamp in the distance, the red to the left I am not sure.

Page 53:- Lots of red energy, in the middle it looks like a bird flying, to the far left it looks like a flying horse / unicorn.

Page 54:- Me holding my baby niece to the left, my brother with an angelic being sitting on him watching the baby. This was taken on night mode as this sometimes helped see if there was anything there, sometimes I would just know what programme to use.

Page 56:- The wheel I was guided to make, each crystal represents each of the fifteen Archangels I have written about as do the coloured ribbons. There is angelic energy flowing on up through the wheel. To the left is colours of items that was lifted by the energy.

Page 69:- There was an unwanted energy in the house this night and my angel came through the window to the right to help me.

Descriptions for the Photograph's (continued)

Page 79:- I asked my angel if she would stand in front of me so I could take a photo and she did. I am actually sitting on the settee behind the image.

Page80:- The remains of aura as my angel goes past me after taking her photo.

Page 81:- Another time when my angel was making her presence known.

Page 86:- Around 11pm, me in bed talking to my angel, I faced the camera at arms length towards me and took this photo.

Page 87:- Another photo of me and my angel talking in my bedroom.

Page 90:- The ceiling in my living room, this looks like an angel and all her colours, plenty of angelic energy around. The ceiling is white and the walls are pale lilac normally.

Page 91:- This photo was taken in September 2008. The rowan tree in the background covered in angelic energy as is the small bush, the golden orb is seen here on the tree but is partly faded.

Page 93:- Me, new year 2008 not long after midnight, there are small Christmas lights way on the house in the background but angelic energy obviously made these colours and shapes dance in front of my face.

Descriptions for the Photograph's (continued)

Page 99:- October 2008, the full moon, I opened my back door and got this angelic energy with orbs appearing.

Page 100:- Going round the back garden the angelic energy came over the house.

Page 101:- I stood by the rowan tree under the full moon talking to the Angels and all these orbs appeared. Just Amazing…

Love e Blessings
Susan Cormack

Join me on Facebook, Instagram
my Yutobe Channel.
susancormack7@hotmail.co.uk

Lightning Source UK Ltd.
Milton Keynes UK
UKHW050645081119
353116UK00002B/16/P